Pont Aberglaslyn

FAVOURITE WELSH RECIPES

compiled by
Sheila Howells

with illustrations
by A.R.Quinton

SALMON

*I*NDEX

Cover pictures: *front* Earl Lloyd George's Birthplace, Llanystumdwy
back The Swallow Falls, Betws-y-Coed

Printed and Published by J. Salmon Ltd., Sevenoaks, England ©

GLAMORGAN SAUSAGES

4 oz. strong Cheddar cheese, grated
4 oz. fresh white breadcrumbs
1 small onion, finely chopped
1 teaspoon dry mustard powder
1 tablespoon chopped parsley
A pinch of thyme
Salt and pepper
2 small eggs
1 large egg
Dried breadcrumbs for coating
Oil for frying

In a bowl beat the two small eggs and add the mustard, parsley, thyme and seasoning. In a separate bowl mix together the cheese, breadcrumbs and the onion. Now combine the egg mixture with the breadcrumb mixture. With floured hands form the mixture into approximately 10 sausage-shaped rolls. Beat the large egg in a bowl, dip in the sausages, coat them with the dry breadcrumbs and fry in oil until golden brown. Drain well. Serve with a crunchy green salad.

The Viaduct and Cader Idris, Barmouth

WELSH CAKES – *PICE AR Y MAEN*

1 lb. flour
1 teaspoon baking powder
1 pinch allspice
1 pinch salt
4 oz. butter
4 oz. lard
7 oz. sugar
4 oz. seedless raisins
2 eggs, beaten
Milk to mix
Caster sugar to sprinkle

Stir together the flour, baking powder, allspice and salt in a large bowl. Rub in the butter and lard. Add the sugar and raisins. Beat the eggs and add to the mixture, with a little milk, to make a fairly stiff dough. Roll out to a thickness of about ¼ inch and cut into 2 inch rounds with a pastry cutter. Cook on a greased griddle or heavy based frying pan for about 3 minutes each side until golden brown. Sprinkle with sugar and serve warm.

Dee Salmon Fish Cakes

8 oz. poached salmon, finely flaked
1 lb. potatoes, peeled
3 oz. butter
1 tablespoon parsley, chopped
1 tablespoon chives, chopped
Salt and pepper
Zest of ½ lemon
Oil for frying

Boil the potatoes until tender. Mash well with 1 oz. of butter and mix in the finely-flaked salmon, the chopped parsley, chopped chives and lemon zest. Season to taste with salt and pepper. Turn out on to a floured surface, divide into 8 portions and shape into cakes. Fry in 2 oz. of butter mixed with oil until golden brown on each side. Drain on kitchen paper. Serve as a starter on a bed of lettuce with soured cream and chive dressing or as a main course garnished with parsley and lemon wedges.

TEISEN LAP

½ lb. plain flour
1 pinch salt
1 teaspoon baking powder
1 pinch nutmeg
4 oz. butter
2 oz. caster sugar
4 oz. currants
2 eggs, well beaten
¼ pint milk

Set oven to 350°F or Mark 4. Grease a shallow baking tin. Sieve the flour, salt, baking powder and nutmeg into a bowl. Rub in the butter and mix in the sugar and the currants. Beat the eggs well and mix into the dry ingredients. Add the milk slowly and beat well to make a soft dough. Pour the mixture into the tin and bake for 30–40 minutes until light golden brown.

Welsh Faggots

1 lb. pig's liver
2 medium onions
3 oz. shredded suet
4 oz. fresh breadcrumbs
1 teaspoon fresh sage
(or ½ teaspoon dried sage)
Salt and pepper
½ pint beef stock

Set oven to 350°F or Mark 4. Mince the liver and onion together, preferably in a food processor. Put in a bowl and stir in the suet, breadcrumbs, sage and seasoning to taste. Form the mixture into 12 balls with floured hands and place in a well-greased, shallow ovenproof dish. Pour the stock into the dish. Cover and bake for about 30 minutes. Uncover and continue cooking for a further 10 minutes or so to brown the faggots. The remaining gravy may then be thickened, if preferred. Serve with creamed potatoes. Serves 6.

Conwy Castle

LEMON CHEESE

8 oz. caster sugar
5 oz. butter
2 large eggs
2 lemons

Grate the lemons finely to remove the zest only and squeeze the juice from the lemons. Put the sugar and butter in a double saucepan over boiling water. Blend the sugar and butter together over the simmering water until the sugar has dissolved. Beat the eggs lightly and add the lemon mixture. Stir and add this mixture to the double saucepan. Heat slowly until the mixture thickens. Do not over cook. This mixture will coat the back of a wooden spoon when ready. Pour into small, sterilised pots and allow to set. Cover when cold and refrigerate until ready to use.

TREACLE SCONES

12 oz. self-raising light wholemeal flour
3 oz. butter
1 dessertspoon black treacle
½ teaspoon salt
7 oz. milk, (approximately)

Set oven to 400°F or Mark 6. Add the salt to the flour in a mixing bowl and rub in the butter until the mixture resembles bread crumbs. Stir in the treacle and enough milk to make a soft dough. Roll out gently on a floured surface to about 1–1¼ inches in thickness and cut into rounds with a 2 inch pastry cutter. Place on a greased and floured baking tray and bake at the top of the oven for 10–15 minutes. Cool on a wire tray. Serve the scones cut in half and buttered; they are delicious with lemon cheese.

North Sands, Tenby

Laverbread Cakes – *BARA LAWR*

1 lb. laverbread (fresh or bottled)
4 oz. fine oatmeal
6 rashers bacon

Mix the laverbread and oatmeal together and form the mixture into small, round, flatish cakes. Fry the prepared cakes in hot fat (preferably bacon fat) using a palette knife to keep them in shape. Fry until they are crisp and brown on both sides. Serve with the grilled rashers of bacon as a breakfast dish.

Laver is a red-coloured, edible seaweed that grows on the Welsh coast. If bought fresh it must be very well washed to remove all sand and then boiled for 5–6 hours. When cooked it is minced or chopped and at this stage it becomes laverbread.

Welsh Rarebit

4 slices of bread
1 oz. butter, softened
1 level teaspoon made mustard
¼ level teaspoon salt
A shake of Cayenne pepper
¼ teaspoon Worcestershire sauce
6 oz. Cheddar cheese, grated
2 tablespoons milk or beer

In a bowl cream the butter well and stir in the mustard, salt, Cayenne pepper, Worcestershire sauce, cheese and milk or beer. Toast the slices of bread on one side only, spread the mixture on the un-toasted side and brown under a hot grill.

A Buck Rarebit is the same as above but served with a poached egg on top.

Gwent Gooseberry Cream

1 lb. gooseberries
¾ oz. caster sugar
8 oz. double cream
5 oz. plain yoghurt
A few drops vanilla essence
1 teaspoon icing sugar
6 dessertspoons demarara sugar

Poach the gooseberries in a saucepan with the caster sugar; keep them whole by poaching gently; add more sugar if preferred. Cool. Spoon the gooseberries, in a little juice, into 6 ramekin dishes. Beat the yoghurt and cream together until they form soft peaks, fold in the vanilla essence and the icing sugar and spoon the mixture on top of the gooseberries. Sprinkle a dessertspoon of demarara sugar over the top of each remekin. Cover with cling film and refrigerate for several hours. The sugar forms a nice crunchy topping.

Honeyed Welsh Lamb – oen cymreig melog

4 lb. leg of lamb
6 tablespoons Welsh clover honey
Sprig of rosemary
Salt and freshly ground pepper
½ pint cider

Set oven to 400°F or Mark 6. Place the leg of lamb on kitchen foil in a roasting tin. Brush with 4 tablespoons of warm honey and season with salt and pepper. Place the sprig of rosemary on top of the joint. Draw up the foil to form a tent and roast for 15 minutes. Lower the heat to 350°F or Mark 4 and continue roasting for 1½ hours until the juice just runs pink or longer if preferred well done. Open up the foil to crisp and brown the skin for the last 20 minutes of cooking time. Remove the lamb from the oven and keep warm. Pour off the fat from the pan and make the gravy from the meat residue, adding half a pint of cider and 2 tablespoons of honey. Reduce to two thirds by boiling. Serve with roast potatoes and green vegetables.

The Bridge, Beddgelert

TREACLE TOFFEE

2 oz. butter
8 oz. demarara sugar
4 oz. black treacle
4 oz. golden syrup

Grease a shallow tin 6 inches x 4 inches approximately. Melt the butter, sugar, treacle and syrup in a heavy based saucepan. Stir until the sugar has dissolved. Then increase the heat slightly and boil, without stirring, until crack point is reached (310°F on a sugar thermometer or when a few drops of toffee dropped into a bowl of cold water separates into brittle threads). Pour into the greased toffee tin and leave in a cool place to set. Mark into squares while still warm and, when set, break into pieces with a toffee hammer.

LLANDUDNO FRUIT CAKE

8 oz. butter
4 oz. caster sugar
4 eggs, separated
1 teaspoon grated orange rind
1 teaspoon grated cinnamon
4 oz. ground almonds
2 oz. ground rice
12 oz. self-raising flour
8 oz. raisins, finely chopped
4 oz. currants, finely chopped
2 oz. glacé cherries
finely chopped
4 oz. sultanas, finely chopped

Set oven to 350°F or Mark 4. Grease and line a 9 inch cake tin. Cream the butter and sugar together in a mixing bowl until light and fluffy then break in the egg yolks, the orange rind and the cinnamon. Mix the ground almonds and ground rice into the flour and then add this, a little at a time, to the creamed mixture, alternating with handfuls of the fruit. Beat well after each addition. Whip the egg whites until stiff and fold carefully into the mixture. Turn the mixture into the cake tin and bake for half an hour. Reduce the heat to 325°F or Mark 3 and cook for approximately 2 more hours; the cake is cooked when a skewer pushed into the centre comes out clean. Cool in the tin then turn out on to a wire rack. Leave until quite cold.

LLANDRINDOD WELLS
THE PARISH CHURCH.

A.R.QUINTON

The Parish Church, Llandrindod Wells

Cawl

2 lb. neck of Welsh lamb
3 pints lamb or vegetable stock
½ lb. peas, shelled
½ lb. broad beans, shelled
1 small cauliflower, broken into florets
1 medium leek, diced
1 medium carrot, diced
1 medium onion, diced
1 medium turnip, diced
1 medium parsnip, diced
2–3 lettuce leaves, shredded
Salt and pepper
Chopped parsley to garnish

Trim the lamb to remove the fat. Place the meat in a saucepan with a very little cooking oil and brown on all sides. Cover with stock and bring to the boil, skimming if necessary. Prepare all the vegetables and set aside the cauliflower and lettuce until later. Add the rest of the vegetables to the meat and season with salt and pepper. Cover and simmer for 2½–3 hours. Add the cauliflower and lettuce to the broth 20 minutes before the end of the cooking time. Sprinkle with chopped parsley and serve piping hot with crusty bread.

CRUNCHY CRAB CREAMS

1 oz. butter
1 oz. flour
½ pint milk
2 tablespoons single cream
½ teaspoon ground mace
Salt and pepper
½ lb. white crab meat, fresh or frozen
2 tablespoons soured cream
2 oz. fresh white breadcrumbs
1 tablespoon finely grated cheese
Extra butter

Set oven to 400°F or Mark 6. In a saucepan make a roux with 1 oz. butter and 1 oz. flour. Add the milk and single cream to make a white sauce. Stir in the mace and season with salt and pepper. Mix in the crab meat and the soured cream, return to the heat and bring to the boil. Spoon the mixture into 6 ramekins, sprinkle with breadcrumbs and the grated cheese and, finally, dot with butter. Stand in a *bain marie* and bake for 10 minutes until crisp and golden brown. Serve with crusty bread or Melba toast, as a starter.

Gwilym's Favourites

4 oz. butter
4 oz. caster sugar
5 oz. flour
1 teaspoon orange zest
2 oz. chopped walnuts

Set oven to 350°F or Mark 4. Cream the butter and sugar in a mixing bowl until light and fluffy. Fold in the flour, orange zest and chopped walnuts to form a stiff dough. Place in small heaps on greased, floured baking trays. Bake for 10–15 minutes until golden brown. Remove from the trays and cool on a wire rack. Makes about 20 buns.

Snowdon Pudding – PWDIN ERYRI

2 oz. raisins
4 oz. suet
Pinch of salt
4 oz. fresh breadcrumbs
Grated rind of 2 lemons
1½ oz. ground rice or cornflour
3 oz. soft brown sugar
3 eggs
3 oz. lemon marmalade

Butter a 1 pint pudding basin. Cover the base with raisins. Mix all the dry ingredients together in a bowl. Beat the eggs and add to the mixture with the marmalade. Pour into the basin and cover with greaseproof paper and kitchen foil. Steam for 1½ hours. Serve with a pouring custard.

Snowdon from Capel Curig

Stuffed Herrings

4 medium-sized herrings, boned and
with heads and tails removed
1 medium onion, finely chopped
2 oz. fresh breadcrumbs
2 oz. walnuts, chopped
1 tablespoon made mustard
Juice and zest of one lemon
3 tablespoons fresh herbs, chopped
(i.e. parsley, chives, thyme)
2 oz. butter
Salt and pepper

Melt a knob of butter in a saucepan and soften the onion. Mix the breadcrumbs, chopped walnuts, mustard, lemon zest and mixed herbs in a bowl and add the onion and about a tablespoon of lemon juice and bind together. Stuff each herring with this mixture. Fold over and close neatly. Make three cuts on each side at the thick end of each fish to ensure even cooking. Melt the butter in frying pan and fry the fish for about 10 minutes, turning them once. They should be tender and nicely browned. Pour on the remaining lemon juice and serve with creamed potatoes and vegetables in season.

Boiled Bacon with Orange and Port

1 bacon joint, 3–4 lbs.
1 oz. butter
1oz. flour
½ pint vegetable stock
2 tablespoons orange juice
1 teaspoon grated orange zest
¼ pint port wine
¼ teaspoon freshly ground black pepper
¼ teaspoon redcurrant jelly
Pinch of salt

Soak the bacon overnight in cold water to remove salt, if appropriate. Next day discard the water, cover with fresh cold water, bring to the boil and skim. Cooking time 30 minutes to each pound of bacon. For the sauce, melt the butter in a saucepan, add the flour and stir well to make a roux. Add the stock and stir until the sauce is thick and smooth. Stir in the orange juice, orange zest, port wine and pepper. Add the red-currant jelly and stir until it is melted. Add salt to taste. Drain the bacon and slice. Arrange the slices on a serving dish and serve the sauce separately with roast or new potatoes and buttered carrots. Serves 6–8.

Torrent Walk, Dolgellau

BARA BRITH

10 oz. mixed fruit
⅔ pint hot tea
3 oz. soft brown sugar
Grated rind of 1 lemon
12 oz. self-raising wholemeal flour
1 teaspoon mixed spice
1 large egg

Soak the mixed fruit in the hot tea, cover and leave to stand overnight. Next day set oven to 350°F or Mark 4, and grease and line a 2 lb. loaf tin. Strain the fruit and reserve the liquid. Mix together the fruit with the other ingredients in a bowl, adding the reserved liquid a little at a time until a soft dropping consistency is achieved. Pour the mixture into the tin and bake for 45–55 minutes until risen and firm to the touch. Cool and serve sliced and buttered.

Auntie Maria's Whinberry Tart

8 oz. flour
A little salt
1 oz. cornflour
2 teaspoons caster sugar
4 oz. butter
1 egg yolk
2 tablespoons water
1 lb. whinberries, (or blueberries)
fresh, frozen or bottled
4 oz. icing sugar
2 eggs
3 oz. ground almonds
Almond essence, if desired

Set oven to 400°F or Mark 6. Sift the flour, salt, cornflour and caster sugar into a mixing bowl. Rub in the butter until the mixture resembles fine breadcrumbs. Add the egg yolk and 2 tablespoons of cold water and bind together. Roll out on a lightly floured surface and line a 9 inch flan dish. Bake blind for 10 minutes or so, until beginning to firm. Spread the whinberries over the bottom of the flan case (if the whinberries are bottled, drain off the liquid; thaw if frozen). Mix together the icing sugar, eggs, almonds and a drop of almond essence, if desired. Pour this mixture over the whinberries and bake at 325°F or Mark 3 for 45–55 minutes until golden brown. Serve hot or cold, with pouring cream.

Brecon Light Cakes

4 oz. self-raising flour
½ teaspoon salt
2 oz. caster sugar
2 eggs
2 tablespoons orange juice
2–3 tablespoons milk
1 oz. margarine for frying
1 oz. soft brown sugar

Beat the eggs together with half the orange juice. Sift the flour and the salt into a mixing bowl and add the caster sugar. Add the egg mixture, stirring well. Beat in the milk to produce a fairly thin batter. Melt the margarine in a heavy frying pan. When it begins to sizzle, drop in tablespoons of the mixture, allowing room to spread (2–3 inches). Cook on each side until golden brown. Drain on kitchen paper. Serve sprinkled with brown sugar and orange juice.

Monmouth Pudding – PWDIN MYNWY

1 oz. butter
1 oz. sugar
¾ pint milk
Grated rind of 1 lemon
6 oz. fresh white breadcrumbs
3 egg yolks
4–5 tablespoons strawberry jam

Set oven to 350°F or Mark 4. Put the milk in a saucepan and add the butter, sugar and grated lemon rind and bring to the boil. Put the breadcrumbs in a bowl and pour the hot milk mixture over them. Allow to cool and swell. Stir the egg yolks into the cooled mixture and then spread half into a greased, ovenproof dish. Melt the jam, pour half of it over the mixture, add the remaining breadcrumbs mixture and finish with a layer of jam. Bake for 40–45 minutes until set.

Tintern Abbey

STONE CREAM

1 lb. tin of apricots (drained)
2 tablespoons soft brown sugar
1 tablespoon brandy or sherry
½ oz. gelatine
2 tablespoon warm water
1 pint single cream
2 oz. icing sugar

Spread the apricots over the bottom of a glass serving bowl and sprinkle with the soft brown sugar and the brandy or sherry. Dissolve the gelatine in the warm water, according to the packet. Put the cream in a heavy saucepan and bring to the boil, stirring in the icing sugar meanwhile. When the cream mixture has just boiled add the gelatine, stirring well. Allow to cool and pour over the mixture in the serving bowl. Chill before serving.

LEEK AND CHEESE FLAN

10 oz. shortcrust pastry
2 large leeks
Oil or butter to sauté the leeks
3 large eggs
3 fl oz. milk
3 fl oz. soured cream
A pinch of salt
6 oz. Cheddar cheese, grated
Ground nutmeg

Set oven to 400°F or Mark 6. Line a 9 inch flan tin with the pastry. Slice the washed leeks and sauté them in a pan until they are just soft; season with black pepper and cool. Whisk together the eggs, milk, soured cream and a pinch of salt and then add half the cheese and the leeks to this mixture. Pour into the flan case and sprinkle the remainder of the cheese over the top. Grate some nutmeg over, place on a pre-heated baking sheet in the oven and bake for ½ an hour until golden brown.

The Menai Bridge

ANGLESEY EGGS – WYAU YNYS MON

6 small leeks, chopped and cooked
1 lb. of hot mashed potatoes
3 oz. butter
Salt and black pepper
1 tablespoon of flour
½ pint hot milk
3 oz. Cheddar cheese, grated
8 hard boiled eggs, halved
2 tablespoons fresh breadcumbs
Grated nutmeg

Set oven to 350°F or Mark 4. Combine the leeks, mashed potatoes and half the butter; season and beat well together. Place in a buttered, ovenproof dish. Make a cheese sauce by melting 1 oz. of butter in a small pan, add the flour, stir and cook for 2 minutes over a low heat. Stir in the milk, add the cheese and simmer, stirring, until it thickens (reserve half an ounce of butter and a little cheese for sprinkling over the finished dish). Arrange the halved hard boiled eggs over the potato and leek mixture. Pour the cheese sauce over. Mix the remaining cheese with the breadcrumbs and sprinkle over the sauce; dot with the remaining butter and grate a little nutmeg over. Bake for 15–20 minutes until nicely browned. Serve with broccolli or peas.

CINNAMON CAKE – TEISEN SINAMON

8 oz. self-raising flour
1 teaspoon ground cinnamon
Pinch of salt
4 oz. butter
4 oz. caster sugar
3 eggs, separated
A little milk to moisten
1 tablespoon golden caster sugar
Raspberry or strawberry jam

Set oven to 350°F or Mark 4. Grease a shallow 8 inch or similar baking tin. Sieve together in a bowl the flour, cinnamon and pinch of salt. Rub in the butter. Add the caster sugar and the beaten egg yolks to the flour mixture and mix well to a fairly stiff consistency. Add sufficient milk to moisten slightly. Turn the mixture into the tin and bake for about 25 minutes until cooked through. Turn out and cool on a wire rack. Reduce oven temperature to 325°F or Mark 3. For the topping, whip the egg whites until stiff and fold in the golden caster sugar. Spread jam over the top of the cake and then pile on the meringue mixture. Return to the oven and cook for about 20 minutes until the meringue is set and pale golden brown. This dessert is best eaten straight away.

Potato Bakes

2 large potatoes, scrubbed
1 leek, chopped
4 rashers of bacon, chopped
2 oz. cream cheese
Salt and pepper
1 oz. Cheddar cheese, grated

Bake the potatoes in the oven for as long as may be necessary. Remove, cool a little and cut in half. Sweat the leek in a saucepan with the bacon for a few minutes; the bacon fat should be sufficient. Carefully scoop out the centres of the potatoes from the skins into a bowl, mash and add the cream cheese and the leek and bacon together with salt and pepper to taste. Pile back into the skins, top with grated cheese and grill until golden brown and bubbly. Serves 2.

BREAST OF DUCK WITH WHINBERRY SAUCE

6 duck breasts, 6–7 oz. each
1 tablespoon honey, warmed and
mixed together with
1 tablespoon lemon juice
¼ pint poached Whinberries
(or blueberries) fresh
frozen or bottled
¼ pint ruby port wine
2 tablespoons lemon juice
1 heaped tablespoon arrowroot
2 tablespoons water

Set oven to 350°F or Mark 4. Prick the duck breast skins all over and place them on a wire rack in a roasting tin. Brush with the lemon/honey mixture. Season with salt and black pepper and roast for approximately 30 minutes until crisp and cooked through. In the meantime make the sauce. Put the port wine and the two tablespoons of lemon juice in a saucepan, and bring the mixture to the boil. Mix the arrowroot with 2 tablespoons of water, add to the pan and thicken the mixture. Then add the Whinberries, (if the whinberries are bottled, drain off the liquid; thaw if frozen). Bring to the boil again, stirring carefully. Serve in a sauceboat separately with creamed or roast potatoes and green vegetables. Serves 6.

Harlech Castle

CREAM OF LEEK SOUP

1 oz. butter
4 rashers of streaky bacon, chopped
4 large leeks, chopped
1 lb. potatoes, peeled and chopped
1½ pints chicken stock
¼ pint milk
Salt and pepper
2 tablespoons cream

Melt the butter and soften the bacon and leeks together in large saucepan and then add the potatoes. Pour on the stock and season to taste. Bring to the boil and simmer for about 30 minutes. When the mixture is soft, rub through a sieve or liquidize in a food processor. Add the milk and cream, re-heat but *do not* boil and serve garnished with chopped parsley. Croutons or sippets may be served separately.

Penbryn Cheese Pudding

4 oz. Penbryn cheese, grated
(Cheddar cheese is an
acceptable substitute)
3 oz. fresh breadcrumbs
1 oz. butter
2 eggs
Salt and pepper
½ pint milk
Good pinch of dry mustard

Set oven to 350°F or Mark 4. Separate the eggs and beat the yolks lightly in a mixing bowl. Warm the milk and add to the eggs, together with the butter and a pinch of mustard. Mix well and add the breadcrumbs and most of the cheese. Season. Whip the egg whites stiffly and fold into the mixture. Pour the mixture into a buttered pie dish and cover with the remaining cheese. Cook for 30–40 minutes until well-risen, golden brown and just set in the middle. Serve with crusty bread. Serves 6–8.

Pen-y-Garreg Dam, Elan Valley

WELSH TROUT IN BACON

4 small to medium fresh trout
4 knobs of butter
4 sprigs of fresh parsley
4 thin slices of lemon
Black pepper
8 rashers smoked streaky bacon
2 tablespoons chives, chopped
2 tablespoons parsley, chopped
A little extra butter

Gut and clean the trout. Pack the cavity of each trout with a knob of butter, a sprig of parsley, a slice of lemon and add a twist of black pepper. Wrap 2 rashers of bacon around each trout and brush with melted butter. Place the fish under a hot grill and cook for 3–4 minutes on each side. Melt a little extra butter with the juices from the fish, add the chopped chives and parsley and pour over each fish. Serve with parsley potatoes, carrots and minted peas.

Sage and Leek Bread

8 oz. strong white flour
8 oz. strong wholemeal flour
1 sachet dried yeast
1 teaspoon salt
Pepper
2 teaspoons fresh sage, chopped
(or 1 teaspoon dried sage)
1 large leek, washed and finely
chopped
1 oz. butter
½ pint tepid milk
1 teaspoon sesame seeds

Set oven to 400°F or Mark 6. Melt the butter in a saucepan and soften the chopped leek gently. Put the flours, salt, dried yeast, pepper and sage in a large bowl. Make a well and pour in the leek, butter and tepid milk. Beat well together until the dough leaves the sides of the bowl clean. Turn out on to a lightly floured surface and knead well for 10 minutes until smooth. Place in a clean bowl. Cover and leave in a warm place for about one hour until it doubles in size. Turn out and knead well again. Divide into two. Shape into rounds and place on a greased baking sheet. Brush with a little milk and sprinkle with sesame seeds. Cover and leave in a warm place to rise until double in size (30–40 minutes). Bake for 30 minutes. When cooked the loaves should be golden brown and sound hollow when tapped on the bottom. Cool on a wire rack.

CAERPHILLY CHEESE AND CHIVE SCONES

8 oz. self-raising flour
Pinch of salt
2 oz. butter
4 oz. Caerphilly cheese, grated
1 tablespoon snipped fresh chives
¼ pint milk

Set oven to 375°F or Mark 5. Put the flour and salt into a mixing bowl and rub in the butter. Stir in half the cheese and the tablespoon of chives. Add the milk and mix to a soft dough. Turn out on to a lightly floured surface and knead, quickly, until smooth. Roll out to 1 inch in thickness, cut into about ten scones with a 2 inch pastry cutter, brush the tops with milk, put on to a greased baking tray and bake for ten minutes until golden brown. Remove from the oven and, *immediately* sprinkle the tops of the scones with the remaining grated cheese and allow it to melt. Serve warm or cold with butter.

METRIC CONVERSIONS

The weights, measures and oven temperatures used in the preceding recipes can be easily converted to their metric equivalents.

Weights

Avoirdupois	Metric
1 oz.	just under 30 grams
4 oz. (¼ lb.)	app. 115 grams
8 oz. (½ lb.)	app. 230 grams
1 lb.	454 grams

Liquid Measures

Imperial	Metric
1 tablespoon (liquid only)	20 millilitres
1 fl. oz.	app. 30 millilitres
1 gill (¼ pt.)	app. 145 millilitres
½ pt.	app. 285 millilitres
1 pt.	app. 570 millilitres
1 qt.	app. 1.140 litres

Oven Temperatures

	°Fahrenheit	Gas Mark	°Celsius
Slow	300	2	140
	325	3	158
Moderate	350	4	177
	375	5	190
	400	6	204
Hot	425	7	214
	450	8	232
	500	9	260

Flour as specified in these recipes refers to Plain Flour unless otherwise described